HIS SPIRIT
Through Me

Poetry Inspired by God

By
Barbara J. Whitener

Copyright © 2007 by Barbara J. Whitener

His Spirit Through Me
by Barbara J. Whitener

Printed in the United States of America

ISBN-13: 978-1-60034-875-4
ISBN-10: 1-60034-875-0

All rights reserved solely by the author. The author guarantees all contents are original and do not infringe upon the legal rights of any other person or work. No part of this book may be reproduced in any form without the permission of the author. The views expressed in this book are not necessarily those of the publisher.

Unless otherwise indicated, Bible quotations are taken from the King James/Amplified Bible Parallel Edition and The NIV Study Bible, 10th Anniversary Edition. Copyright © 1995 by The Zondervan Corporation and the Lockman Foundation.

www.xulonpress.com

Table of Contents

PREFACE ix

SECTION I: INSPIRATIONS 11

A Page of My Life 11

Baby Blessing 12

Children 13

Colors 14

Daily Delivered 16

Dreams 18

Gifts From God 19

God's Gift of Silence 21

God's Green Earth 23

God Is Always There 25

God's Love Will Ease Your Pain 26

Heart of God 28

Heaven to Earth 30

His Spirit Through Me 31

Jesus 33

Like A Child 34

Never Give Up On Love 35

No Matter 37

Promises 38

Seek Ye First 40

The Lord's Work 42

The Spirit of God 44

Tugging At His Coat 46

Where Would We Be Without You? 48

Wisdom 49

Witness 50

Worldly Work 51

SECTION II: LIFE'S EXPERIENCES 53

Apology 53

Friendship 55

Hurting 57

Image 59

Knowing Your Heart 61

Life: Questions or Calm? 63

Marriage 65

One Small Thing 66

Out of Focus 67

Perfect Bride 69

Real Friends 70

Seasons 71

This Feeling 73

Traveling Mercies 74

Wedding Day 75

SECTION III: FAMILY AND FRIENDS 77

A Birthday Wish 77

Another Year 79

As You Go 80

Brother 81

Christopher Smith 82

CJ Smith Jr. 84

CJ's Gift 86

Fourteen Years 88

God's Precious Daughter 90

Lost Time 92

Mom 93

Number 11 95

One More Year 96

Pastors Chris and Carol 97

Sheila 98

Teenage Present 100

The Birthday Party 102

Preface

Giving honor to the Lord Jesus Christ as the head of my life and to my husband, Howard whom always encouraged me to follow my heart and the plan of God for my life.

This book is a compilation of poems that the Lord has blessed me to write over a number of years. Most of the poems were spiritual impartations into my personal struggles in life. Others were blessings and words of inspiration and encouragement that the Lord gave me to uplift other people's lives. The publishing of this book will be a testimony to what obedience to God can produce. I have been encouraged by several of my friends and co-laborers in Christ about these poems becoming a book, but it took the prodding of the Holy Spirit to really instill this book as a reality of God's promises to me.

I hope that all who read these poems will find the wisdom and peace of God that I have found in them.

I would like to also acknowledge a dear friend of mine who has known me for over 20 years now and was one of the first to read some of these poems and encouraged me to pursue the gift that God had given me. Thank you DeVata Davis for always having an encouraging word for me when I needed it, even when you were going through difficult times yourself. You have truly been a blessing in my life; I love you dearly!

All my love to my husband, sons and family!

Barbara Jeanne Whitener

Section I: Inspirations

A Page of My Life

A page of my life is like an open book,
With God as the author, I need no further look.
His words are always perfect,
His thoughts are most divine.
He wants to write them on my heart
One single line at a time.

He's always been there guiding His pen
Though I hadn't always known Him then.
But by His love and mercy great,
He has made my life a bountiful slate.

May I come to know my Author more.
May I show His love forever more.
I give each page of my life to You
For Yours is the will I lean unto.

*"Let us fix our eyes on Jesus,
the author and perfecter of our faith, . . ."
Hebrews 12:2 (NIV)*

Baby Blessing

A baby is a precious gift!
It gives your spirit such a lift!
This gift from God, your pride and joy!
No matter if a girl or boy!

Be thankful for this heavenly treasure!
For nothing can ever match its measure!
This time again, from God be blessed!
And come into His holiest rest!

*"Lo, children are an heritage of the LORD:
and the fruit of the womb is his reward." Psalms 127:3*

Children

The joy and love that children give
We are often unaware.
It brings us peace and happiness
And rids us of all care.

Their laugh, their smile, their innocence
It all comes from the heart.
And if we all take after them,
Our world won't tear apart.

Children are a gift from God
To love, to teach and nurture;
For if we choose neglect instead,
This world will have no future.

So people of all nations listen,
Protect and love and care;
Our children are the life of the world,
Of this remain aware.

*"But Jesus called them unto him, and said,
suffer little children to come unto me, and forbid them not:
for of such is the kingdom of God." Luke 18:16*

Colors

I saw the face of Christ last night,
It lit up all my dreams.
I could not sleep for seeing Him,
His face shone bright as beams.

I saw the face of Christ last night,
His face seemed oh, so near.
However, there was something different
His complexion was not so clear.

I saw the face of Christ last night,
All colors filled His face.
It told me that the Lord, our God
Is Lord of the human race.

The colors changed and flashed so bright,
They never stayed the same.
It was then the meaning became so clear,
Human beings are one and the same.

Look in a mirror, or down the street
What is it that you see?
A rainbow full of human colors,
And a part of you and me.

Your friends and family, you love so true,
Their color you never see.
Put love in your eyes for all the others,
And colorblind you will be.

And when you see the face of Christ,
Don't hassle, or make a fuss.
For Jesus is the Man of all colors,
And He died for all of us.

"All nations whom Thou hast made shall come and worship before Thee, O Lord; and shall glorify thy name."
Psalms 86:9

Daily Delivered

Because we live in Satan's world
And sin is all around.
We need God's grace each day within
To hurl him to the ground!

We ask God once to save us,
His Spirit He did impart.
We need to use that Spirit power
Each day from within our heart.

God's Spirit is a free gift.
It starts small as a mustard seed.
But without the water of His Word
It gets choked by sin's great weed!

We need God's Word, yes every day
To help us through this life.
Without it we will slip and fall
Into daily toil and strife!

So read God's Word, yes every day.
Your joy like a river will flow.
And with His Word you'll be daily delivered.
God's salvation you will always know!

"Who delivered us from so great a death, and doth deliver: in whom we trust that he will yet deliver us;"
2Cor 1:10

Dreams

Dreams are not for the faint of heart,
They take courage and great fortitude.
To follow a dream you need two special things,
You need faith and a strong attitude.

Dreams may be buried or pushed to the side,
But, dreams can never be lost.
For if, we try living without any dreams
Our lives suffer a terrible cost.

Life without dreaming is life without hope
So we must find that dream in our heart.
With encouragement from friends and strength from Our Lord
That dream will set us apart.

So, open your heart let your dream come to life
And there is something you'll always receive.
You'll get joy in your heart and an uplifted smile,
And in yourself you can always believe.

"And it shall come to pass afterward, that I will pour out my spirit upon all flesh; and your sons and your daughters shall prophesy, your old men shall dream dreams, your young men shall see visions:" Joel 2:28

Gifts From God

Everyday that we live is a gift from God,
Every minute that we breathe;
Every flower and creature and friend we have,
God gives us the things that we need.

Every "up" situation is a gift from God,
Every down that we feel is too;
Every smile and laugh and cry we evoke,
God is sharing them, from Him to you.

The gifts in the Bible are promised,
They are listed from front to back;
The gifts in one's daily living
Many people say they seem to lack.

But, I say to you they are not looking,
His gifts are present every day;
From the first breath we take every morning
To the sun going down by the way.

The birds and the bees and the locusts,
The flowers and the trees and the air;
Only God has His hand in all nature,
Only God shares His love everywhere.

continued

So, open up your eyes; look around you,
See the clouds, the rain, and the dew.
And remember that our heavenly Father,
God Almighty has made them for you.

"...*And God said, Behold, I have given you every herb bearing seed, which is upon the face of all the earth, and every tree, in the which is the fruit of a tree yielding seed; to you it shall be for meat.*" Genesis 1:28-29

God's Gift of Silence

We say we want to hear from God,
"Please speak to me! Hear my prayer."
And yet we fill our days with noise,
No silence 'round us anywhere.

We cry, "God, why don't you answer me?"
"Please show me the way to go!"
But we never stand still long enough,
His voice we can never know.

The television, the telephone,
The radio and more.
We "cannot" live without;
Our lives would "be a bore"!

Education; communication;
Religion at it's best.
Cannot compare with Him above,
God's "noise" should calm the rest.

So, stop and turn the TV off,
No music should be played.
For God has spoken more to us
In the silence that He made.

continued

He wants to speak directly
To each and every soul.
To have us listen and respond
Is truly His only goal!

*"but whoever listens to me will live in safety
and be at ease, without fear of harm." Proverbs 1:33(NIV)*

God's Green Earth

When Adam and Eve lived in Eden
It was such a perfect world.
Not bad, nor evil, no dirt or junk
Did clutter His earth bejeweled.

Now sin came first and spread like fire,
Then bad and evil followed suit.
And when we became "civilized",
Dirt and junk covered every boot.

We now have Earth Day; recycle is a must,
Yet, in a fog some people still thrive.
On highways and byways, both near and far,
They dump their garbage as they drive.

Automobiles pollute earth enough,
Yet, for trash they come well equipped.
Ashtrays, compartments and side door storage
Are a must when we buy, lest we've flipped.

So why then do people still litter the ground,
When their cars can help keep it clean?
Cleaning out one car is must faster all round
And it keeps the Lord's earth so green.

"And the earth brought forth grass, and herb yielding seed after his kind, and the tree yielding fruit, whose seed was in itself, after his kind: and God saw that it was good."
Genesis 1:12

God Is Always There

People come into our lives.
From birth until we die;
They bring good times, or even bad,
We often never know why.

Classmates, neighbors, sometimes friends;
Will come and then will go.
Sometimes we gain a lot from them,
Sometimes we just don't know!

But I believe we come and go
To help others, or to get relief;
And if with open eyes we see,
We'll learn! That's my belief.

Yet, even as friends slip in and out,
We laugh, we cry, we care!
Above all others in our lives,
Our God is always there!

*"Let your conversation be without covetousness;
and be content with such things as ye have: for he hath
said, I will never leave thee, nor forsake thee."*
Hebrews 13:5

God's Love Will Ease Your Pain

We go through trials most every day,
We laugh; we cry; we work; we play.
Sometimes the joy can make us high,
The pain can make us want to die!

To avoid the pain, we run and hide,
Or find more work in-house, outside.
We laugh; we joke; we party all night;
No one can see that we're not all right.

We try so hard to outlast the pain,
Then we wonder why we never gain.
We come to a place where we can't go on,
The pain has won; it's brought us down.

The only place to look is up.
The Lord says, "Come, drink from My cup."
"I've suffered and died and felt more pain,
Than the floods from forty days rain!"

"So, bring to me your hurts and sorrow,
From today, yesterday and even tomorrow.
For I love you more than you can know,
With you in the pain I will always go!"

"You must stop running; turning away,
For your pain goes with you both night and day.
Come rest in Me, I'll give you peace!
I'll walk you through to your final release."

"For My arms are large, and open wide;
My love for you I can not hide.
Only I can stop the wind and rain.
My Love will help to ease your pain!"

"And God shall wipe away all tears from their eyes; and there shall be no more death, neither sorrow, nor crying, neither shall there be any more pain: for the former things are passed away."
Revelations 21:4

Heart of God

H is for the humbleness with which we all should live.

E is for the excellence of God toward which we all should strive.

A is for His Almighty Presence in which we all should walk.

R is for His Righteousness of which we all should talk.

T is for the Truth of Him to all we should truly tell.

O is for the Holy One Who springs an eternal well.

F is for faithfulness toward God we should always show.

G is for His glory in us that should always be a-glow!

O is for His overwhelming love for every living soul.

D is for us to demonstrate Him, in life that is our goal!

To have a heart of God takes time
And effort to obtain.
By seeking God both night and day
That knowledge we will gain.

To truly know the heart of God
Would surely be more than nice.
But remember this, I pray thee,
You must be willing to pay the price!

For although God's love and grace are free
His wisdom's not freely given.
It will take a disciple's mind-set
And sacrificial daily living.

So if you want to know God's heart
Read daily and study His Word.
And humble yourself on your knees each day
And make him your everlasting Lord!

*"And the multitude of them that believed
were of one heart and of one soul:"
Acts 4:32a*

Heaven to Earth

From heaven to earth, God sent His Son.
Through Him to God, the only One.
He came to earth to forgive our sin.
All hearts and souls to truly win.

In heaven, He reigned beside Our Lord!
To earth, He came with just a Word.
He came to die, to set us free!
He came to earth for you and me!

He came to live a lowly life,
He lived to be The Sacrifice.
He came to earth to be with man.
He came to earth, The Holy Lamb!

With just a Word, from heaven He came,
To live, to love, to die in pain.
But into heaven He arose!
To come again: when? No one knows.

But this we know, from heaven He'll reign,
And claim the earth as His again!

"For I came down from heaven, not to do mine own will, but the will of him that sent me." John 6:38

His Spirit Through Me

God has given me words to write.
They come in the day and sometimes at night.
God has given the words to say,
To help someone come follow His Way.

The words that come, are first meant for me,
To help, His meaning of life, that I see.
He reveals words, each verse in my mind,
Amazing to me is they come right on time.

His words offer comfort, and sometimes explain,
Why sometimes we suffer and sometimes we gain.
The words tell a story of life as we grow,
And how the Lord guides us, through life, to and fro.

He shows us our faults; He supplies all our needs,
And when we stumble, oh, how His heart bleeds.
But God is forgiving, He loves us and yet;
Satan deceives us and makes us forget.

So, if God is willing, more words He will send,
To help broken hearts and lives on the mend.
I pray to the Lord, and He'll answer this plea,
'Make me humble, oh Lord, send Your Spirit through me.'

continued

*"But when the Comforter is come, whom I will send unto
you from the Father, even the Spirit of truth,
which proceedeth from the Father, he shall testify of me:"
John 15:26*

Jesus

J is for our judgment God laid upon His life.

E is for Emanuel, God [is] with us all the time.

S is for the suffering He endured for our sake.

U is for His unconditional love, from us no one can take.

S is for Salvation that He gave to you and me.

Won't you accept this Jesus so your life can be made free!

"And she shall bring forth a son, and thou shalt call his name JESUS: for he shall save his people from their sins."
Matthew 1:21

Like A Child

Like a child, we should be,
When we come to be with Thee.
We should ask You what to do,
In all things, old and new.

Like a child, we should run,
To You Father, and Your Son.
With Your arms open wide,
We can safely come and hide!

Like a child, there is no shame,
When we call on Jesus Name.
With His love there is no other:
Brother, sister, father, mother.

Like a child to the kingdom come,
His loving arms are safe and warm.
Entering in, a simple thing,
Like a child, come to the King!

"Whosoever therefore shall humble himself as this little child, the same is greatest in the kingdom of heaven."
Matthew 18:4

Never Give Up On Love

Life may deal us ups and downs,
It may be cruel and heartless;
But we can overcome it all
And press on through regardless.

The things that we must focus on,
Are the things that count the most;
Our family, friends, but first of all,
The Father, Son and Holy Ghost.

Our lives are riddled with twists and turns,
Decisions on which way to go;
The only way to get through it all,
Is to let God direct the flow.

And one great thing that comes from God
Surrounds all things here and above;
The greatest gift that He can give,
Hallelujah! It's the gift of Love!

So, when you think life is being hard
And it's all just a push or a shove;
Remember, Christ paid for it all,
And never give up on love!

continued

"No man hath seen God at any time. If we love one another, God dwelleth in us, and his love is perfected in us."
1 John 4:12

No Matter

No matter what this world may bring,
No matter what is said;
No matter where we go in life,
Our God is at the head.

No matter if things go our way,
Or turn out like we planned;
No matter if it's up or down,
It's touched by God's own hand.

No matter if we're right or wrong,
Or do things perfectly;
No matter what our friends may say,
His miracles are plain to see.

No matter how our lives turn out,
With many beautiful things;
The matter we should cherish most,
Is that God is King of Kings.

*"God is our refuge and strength,
a very present help in trouble." Psalms 46:1*

Promises

God made us promises,
In the Bible you can read.
He promised He'd be with us
And supply our every need.

God made us promises,
In the Bible it does tell.
He said He'd light our path with vision
And lift us each time we fell.

God made us promises,
Read the Bible, I implore.
He said that if we thank Him now,
He'll give us so much more.

God made us promises,
And this I know as fact.
Your faith in Him, if tenfold
He'll give all, and more, right back.

God made us promises,
I can't be more secure.
And with the faith of a mustard seed,
Your future He will ensure.

"Whereby are given unto us exceeding great and precious promises: that by these ye might be partakers of the divine nature, . . ."
2 Peter 1:4

Seek Ye First

We start out saying, "Yes Lord, Yes",
We want to do Your will.
We jump, we clap, we shout for joy,
We're glad to climb Your hill.

This attitude may last a week,
A month, a year or two;
But then a change comes over us
And we look away from You.

We begin to ask, "What can we do?"
To help promote His cause.
We try; we fail, and try again
Without coming to a pause.

After frustration begins to mount
And our spirit says stop and rest.
We ask the Lord; "What's wrong with me?"
"I've tried and tried my best!"

We cry and cry; our spirit's athirst
The Lord says "Please calm down!"
"I told you once to Seek Ye First
My Kingdom and all things will come!"

The Lord wants all to seek Him first,
About nothing should we ever travail.
For the Lord our God assures us
That His grace and mercy will prevail.

"But seek ye first the kingdom of God, and his righteousness; and all these things shall be added unto you."
Matthew 6:33

The Lord's Work

The people of this world of ours,
Live for their jobs each day;
They fight the traffic to and fro
To earn their weekly pay.

The people of this world of ours,
Are fiercely competitive;
They run to meet a deadline,
Yet are forgetting how to live.

The people of this world of ours,
Need to stop and realize,
Just what should be important
In the living of their lives.

The people of this world of ours,
Need to heed the Word of God;
And live for Jesus Christ the Lord,
And shout His praise out loud.

For if the people of this world
Will focus on His Word;
The chaos of this daily life
Will die upon the Sword.

So, people of this world of ours,
May be looked at with a quirk;
By living life for Jesus Christ,
You're fulfilling the Lord's Work.

*"I have glorified thee on the earth:
I have finished the work which thou gavest me to do"*
John17:4

The Spirit of God

Have you ever felt the Spirit of God
When it comes into the room?
Have you ever felt the Spirit of God
As it takes away the gloom?

Have you ever felt the Spirit of God
Filling up a holy place?
Have you ever felt the Spirit of God
As it brightens a sinners' face?

Have you ever felt the Spirit of God
With wisdom it does impart?
Have you ever felt the Spirit of God
As it warms a once frozen heart?

Have you ever felt the Spirit of God
Lift your spirit and give it flight?
Have you ever felt the Spirit of God
Dry up a cold, rainy night?

Have you ever felt the Spirit of God
Give your soul never ending peace?
Have you ever felt the Spirit of God?
If not, you must give it release.

The Spirit of God is a gift to all,
Just accept is all we need do.
Simply say, "Yes, Lord I want it",
Peace and joy will come right now to you.

*"Through mighty signs and wonders,
by the power of the Spirit of God;"*
Romans 15:19a

Tugging At His Coat

We come to Him as little children
With our hearts and eyes all aglow;
We want to see Him, touch Him, feel Him,
His wisdom, All; we want to know.

So when He speaks we ask Him, Why?
And the answers He does give;
Yet in His time, and not our own,
Life seems to slip away through a sieve.

Then we ask Him again; Please answer,
And tugging at His coat we plea;
'Dear Lord won't you teach me much faster?'
Yet, He waits for His time so patiently.

Like our children, we keep asking over and over,
And we think that our voice He mustn't hear;
Then we tug once more on the hem of His coat
Just to let Him know we're still there.

As a child, we come to our breaking point,
So we tug and we scream and we cry;
And He turns and looks at us calmly,
And He patiently and simply says; "Why?"

"My child I have given you answers,
To many questions throughout the years;
Some that you didn't have to ask for,
And others that you begged for through tears."

"So why now do you grow so impatient?
An answer you know you will get.
I haven't forsaken you, ever,
And every need that you had I have met."

"So please my dear child, stop tugging,
Your prayers and your pleas I have heard.
I will give you all that you have asked for,
That's a promise I gave in My Word."

"And besought him that they might only touch the hem of his garment: and as many as touched were made perfectly whole." Matthew 14:36

Where Would We Be Without You?

Where would we be without You?
Where would we be, Lord?
Lost in our sin without You!
Where would we be, Lord?

You came to give us life!
You came to take our strife!
You came so we won't die!
Where would we be, Lord?
Where would we be?

*"For the Son of man is come to seek
and to save that which was lost." Luke19:10*

Wisdom

Wisdom doesn't come from books,
Or teachers back at school;
Wisdom comes from but one place,
The same as the Golden Rule.

Love thy neighbor as thyself,
Is simple, yes it's true;
Wisdom is so easy to have,
Love me, as I love you.

Some people want to make it hard
And others just don't care;
The Lord above has made it easy,
Just read the Bible; be aware.

Wisdom comes with life and age,
Immediate knowledge there's not;
But if you live by God's true Word,
Life will follow an easy plot.

"For the LORD giveth wisdom:
out of his mouth cometh knowledge and understanding."
Proverbs 2:6

Witness

Some times we think we need to be
Some big important star;
But all the Lord has asked of us,
Is just to be who we are.

Our lives don't have to be colossal,
Or so bright to cause a glare'
But just to live as Jesus did
Will cause many to stop and stare.

The little things in life are so
Simplistic and easy to start;
And best of all the little things
Will come straight from the heart.

So, if you're worried and full of fear
That your witness will go untoward;
Remember the example of all
Is Jesus Christ, Our Lord.

*"This Jesus hath God raised up,
whereof we all are witnesses." Acts 2:32*

Worldly Work

We go to work each day of the week
With the same thing on our mind;
"Here we go, more problems to attend,
One more day of the same old grind!"

"Nothing seems to work just right",
We moan and gripe and complain.
"We can't enjoy the sunny days,
It might as well just rain!"

Now wait right there; take one step back,
Take a deep breath and relax.
Let's go back to the beginning
And examine all of the facts!

God gave us His one and only Son
To save us from our sin;
Then He placed us here on earth,
Not for work nor pleasure, nor to win.

God gave us life to choose His Son
As our Savior, our deliverance, our grace;
He did not place us on this earth
To win the so-called "Rat-race".

continued

We are alive, but for one cause,
To worship the Lord every day;
Give praise to Him through your worldly work,
Don't let the world lead you astray!

*"For the grace of God that bringeth salvation hath appeared to all men,
Teaching us that, denying ungodliness and worldly lusts, we should live soberly, righteously, and godly, in this present world;" Titus 2:11-12*

Section II: Life's Experiences

Apology

I'm sorry for the words I spoke,
They were cold and heartless and cruel.
I hope your heart I have not broke;
Can you ever forgive this fool?

The words were said without a thought,
You're reaction, I didn't expect.
But I was being a selfish child,
At the time, I thought; "Oh what the heck!"

But after you left, I felt the pain too,
Of betraying a friend, oh so dear.
"What have I done", I thought to myself;
"Please forgive me!" I hope, you will hear.

I know no words can heal the hurt,
As your sister in Christ, I will pray
That with God's grace and a touch of faith,
Soon the wounds I have cut will fade away.

continued

Again, I ask for forgiveness, my friend,
Your love and kindness deserve better.
Let us walk together, again toward God,
And try to follow Christ to the letter.

*"For thou, Lord, art good, and ready to forgive;
and plenteous in mercy unto all them that call upon thee."
Psalms 86:5*

Friendship

Friendship is a special place
Where some have feared to go;
They've shied away, or run and hid,
Afraid to learn, to know.

Some people hide from friendship,
At work they keep furious pace.
It's not the others they run from,
They're afraid of their very own face.

Some people look at friendship
As a challenge or difficult thing;
When truly an honest friendship
Joy and harmony it can bring.

A true and honest friendship
Can help us realize,
That work and deadlines should really be
A very small part of our lives.

So people of this world take heed,
Of a friendship be a part.
For life is much too short, you see,
To live without a caring heart.

continued

*"Greater love hath no man than this,
that a man lay down his life for his friends."
John 15:13*

Hurting

Life is full of many hurts,
Caused by others or self-imposed.
From broken bones and broken dreams,
To broken hearts, God only knows.

The hurting hearts of many souls
Survive this world each day.
We cannot help them all you see,
Only God can make a way.

Be kind; give love to all you meet,
It's the only way to be.
But don't give up your life for one,
Who refuses the truth to see.

The way is paved with peace and grace
For all those who believe.
But only peace and grace can come
To souls willing to receive.

No matter where the hurt began,
No matter win or loose;
Keep on hurting, or run away,
Accept God's peace; you can choose.

continued

"And the peace of God, which passeth all understanding, shall keep your hearts and minds through Christ Jesus."
Phil 4:7

Image

Image is the kind of thing
Some people care about.
But image doesn't mean a thing
If it's simply from without.

The way we look or how we dress
Is superficial, at best.
But what we carry in our hearts
Will overshadow the rest.

A certain look may be nice to have,
But happiness it cannot buy.
So working on your image alone
Is simply working on a lie.

The image that we all should evolve
Is the image of our heart.
If we keep it small and cold inside,
This world will fall apart.

So, when you're looking for an image,
For your heart to fit a mold;
Compare it with the heart of Christ,
It will become as pure as gold.

continued

*So God created man in his own image,
in the image of God created he him;
male and female created he them," Genesis 1:27*

Knowing Your Heart

As human beings we think we're smart,
Education and computers we can handle.
But when it comes to knowing one's heart,
To God we can never hold a candle.

We go through life with our feelings on our sleeve,
And expect our heart no one will break.
Then suddenly, someone we love takes leave,
Through our heart life has run another stake.

As Christians we give our "life" to God,
But as humans we forget two parts.
We hold on tightly to our feelings,
And we continue to cling to our hearts.

God's love is so patient, more than we deserve,
His forgiveness outdoes man's, bar none;
So from His love, Christians must never swerve,
Devotion to Him should never be done.

So, going through life, playing fools with our hearts,
Just remember, God's watching and He cares;
He's been trying to heal us in whole and in parts,
Just let go He can cure all our fears.

*"Wait on the LORD: be of good courage,
and he shall strengthen thine heart. . ."
Psalms 27:14*

Life: Questions or Calm?

Life need not be questioned,
A constant state of worry.
Life does not need rushing,
A constant panic or hurry.

Life is meant to be carefree,
A constant state of peace.
Life is ours to cherish,
A constant state of release.

"How can there be peace?" you ask,
When life is full of pain.
Remember God made a promise,
A rainbow after the rain.

"How can life be simple?" you say,
For trouble is all we perceive.
His yoke is easy, the Bible states,
All we need do is believe.

His peace passes all understanding,
Of this we must take heed.
Our life will be calm and simple
When Our God supplies every need.

*"The LORD will give strength unto his people;
the LORD will bless his people with peace."*
Psalms 29:11

Marriage

Marriage is the unity of spirits,
The joining of two souls.
It's living life together, forever
Through all the joys and tolls.

Marriage is sharing your dreams together.
Encourage some dreams apart.
But all the dreams and all the sharing
Should come straight from the heart.

The joining of two lives is tricky,
Each mate must give and take.
For if one takes without giving,
A loving heart will surely break.

So, share the joy and laughter together,
And work through a few minor pains;
For the sun and flowers of marriage
Can endure and weather the rains.

"Marriage is honourable in all,"
Hebrews 13:4a

One Small Thing

If everyone would take time each day
To do just one small thing;
Like clean a mess, speak kindly to all,
This world with joy would ring.

To pick up some trash, or say "You first",
Or maybe, "Excuse me, please";
Would truly make our lives more pleasant,
We'd float through each day like the breeze.

These things are not that hard to do,
Our children, we teach them with ease.
Why is it then, as adults we forget
To say "Thank You" and to say "Please"?

Can you imagine six billion people
With one small thing to do?
This world would be so sparkling clean,
And peace would always ring true.

*Be kindly affectioned one to another with brotherly love;
in honour preferring one another;"*
Romans 12:10

Out of Focus

As human beings we are amiss
About the things in life.
The things that we should focus on
And the things that bring us strife.

Instead of working toward the future,
We're looking at TV.
Instead of reaching out to help,
We're reaching for "Hi-C".

We need to motivate ourselves
To change the way we live.
Stop looking for what we can take,
Start learning how to give.

The more you give, the more you get,
We've often heard before.
But to put it into practice
Can truly be a chore.

The place to start is simple; yet old,
Great lessons of life held within.
The Bible Testaments, both New and Old
Is where we should begin.

continued

In order to get great things from life
We must learn to freely give.
Not to expect great kudos or thanks,
Yet humbly we must live.

In giving to others, He'll give to us,
Exactly what we need.
God promised His riches in glory
And that's when we'll succeed.

"Finally, brethren, whatsoever things are true, whatsoever things are honest, whatsoever things are just, whatsoever things are pure, whatsoever things are lovely, whatsoever things are of good report; if there be any virtue, and if there be any praise, think on these things."
Philippians 4:8

Perfect Bride

I want to live for Your love Lord.
I want to give my life to You!
I want to be your perfect bride Lord.
So all may see Your love through me.

I grew up watching "Love Boat" on the TV.
And I'd wish that I was all the girl's I'd see.
And for one hour they laughed, they loved and they were romanced. And that was how I thought my life should always be.

When I went out in the world I'd thought I'd found it.
But then it slipped right through my hands most every day.
And when my marriage fell apart I knew I'd lost it.
And that my life would never be the same again.

Then Lord I let You into my life and I began to learn.
That there's so much more to love than what we see!
And now I want to learn much more about Your life Lord.
And truly be the perfect bride that I can be!

"Who can find a virtuous woman?
for her price is far above rubies."
Proverb 31:10

Real Friends

Real friends don't need to be
Around the corner to know;
That through each joy or sorrow
They'll know right where to go.

Real friends can be far apart,
But miles don't mean a thing;
When someone needs a hug or touch,
Just grab the phone; give a ring.

Real friends will always be so close,
You can count on their caring, bar none;
Real friends are connected by more than blood,
By the Father, His Holy Spirit and His Son.

" . . . but I have called you friends;
for all things that I have heard of my Father
I have made known unto you." John 15:15b

Seasons

Seasons come and seasons go,
But do we really see,
The beauty that each season holds,
God's brilliance; so heavenly.

Summer is a time of leisure,
Yet, also the crops do grow;
The richness of life and its simple pleasure,
For this season God's warmth, He does show.

Autumn is a time of change,
The harvest and schooling begin;
The sun, the leaves, the breeze over the range,
Glorious colors our Lord ushers in.

Winter is a time for cold,
Yet darkness and degrees have a reason;
For bears, foxes, trees, young and old
Are at rest in this God given season.

Spring is a time when the world starts anew,
All is fresh and alive, Oh so green!
And through it all we are given a clue
Learning what His seasons really mean.

continued

As the seasons change around you,
Please take the time to see
All the master's perfect miracles
Given freely to you and me.

*"And God said, Let there be lights in the firmament of the
heaven to divide the day from the night;
and let them be for signs, and for seasons,
and for days, and years:"
Genesis 1:14*

This Feeling

This feeling is so overwhelming,
This feeling that I have for you.
I can't describe the way I'm feeling,
Except this feeling is all about you.

The more we talk and share together,
The deeper that this feeling grows.
I can't explain the way I'm feeling,
It seems that only heaven knows.

I want this feeling to grow much stronger.
I want to share it only with you.
This feeling is so overwhelming,
This feeling is that I Love You!

*"But grow in grace, and in the knowledge of
our Lord and Saviour Jesus Christ."*
2Peter 3:18a

Traveling Mercies

I'll miss you dearly as you go,
But there's one thing that you should know;
You've made me laugh and touched my heart,
And sadness will follow when you depart.

But, with God's grace we'll all survive,
And through His mercy we will arrive;
At the places He intends us to go,
And with His peace we will always know.

That through life's travels we can be strong,
Carrying His love to pass along;
So be encouraged and never fret,
For God's still working, He's not through yet!

*"Let thy tender mercies come unto me, that I may live:
for thy law is my delight."
Psalms 119:77*

Wedding Day

The excitement of your wedding day,
It's filled with love and much to say.
The gown, the flowers, the pearls, and more.
You're standing at the marriage door.

But don't forget to take one thing;
God Almighty, Our Lord, Our King!
For when the trials of life flow in,
With Jesus Christ you'll always win!

*"Love is patient, love is kind. It does not envy,
It does not boast, it is not proud. It is not rude, it is not
self-seeking, it is not easily angered, it keeps no record of
wrongs. Love does not delight in evil but rejoices with the
truth. It always protects, always trusts, always hopes,
always perseveres. Love never fails.
And now these three remain: faith, hope, and love.
But the greatest of these is love."
I Corinthians 13:4-8a, 13 (NIV)*

Section III: Family and Friends

A Birthday Wish

There are so many things
That a mother can wish;
For her youngest son
That she truly does miss!

She can wish for love
And warmth that surrounds.
She can wish for joy
And peace that abounds!

She can wish for laughter
To fill the whole earth!
She can wish for you always
To keep that little boy mirth!

But this one wish
Is the best she can give:
With your heart and your soul
For the Lord you will live!

continued

*"For I through the law am dead to the law,
that I might live unto God."
Galatians 2:19*

His Spirit Through Me

Another Year

Another year is almost over,
Another year is done.
Now that you are another year older,
It is time for some birthday fun!

I told you that I bought your present.
I told you that I brought it home.
And you've been asking lots of questions,
While we've talked upon the phone.

Yet, I never told you of my secret,
Not a single hint did I give.
Now, I'll say in Florida it won't be kept,
It stays where cousin Cindy and Mommy live.

"So, what's the present Mom!
Now, you've led me on a hike!"
Well, I'll tell you, my son CJ,
You have a new 10-speed bike!

*"So teach us to number our days,
that we may apply our hearts unto wisdom."
Psalms 90:12*

As You Go

Moving can be a lot of fun,
It can also be a strain.
So as you go, take love and sun
And you will get through all the rain!

Also remember to take the Lord
As you travel to and fro.
And with our prayers and blessings
We will send you as you go

"A faithful man shall abound with blessings:"
Proverbs 28:20a

Brother

Although we rarely speak, or phone,
And we might see each other once a year,
I want you to know you are in my thoughts,
And in my heart, I hold you so dear.

Growing up could be tough at times,
But some fun we surely had.
We may not have "turned out", as we wanted,
But I don't think we turned out half bad!

I want you to know that I love you,
And these words come straight from my heart.
We can still be friends and keep in touch,
Though we're hundreds of miles apart!

So, if you ever want to reminisce
Or just want to blow off some steam,
Remember, we're family, my brother,
I'll be your shoulder to cry on, to dream.

*"And this commandment have we from him,
That he who loveth God love his brother also."
1John 4:21*

Christopher Smith

C is for your cute little face shining bright from morn 'til night.

H is for your happy laugh that keeps away all fright.

R is for your running little legs that only pause for sleep.

I is for the innocence you have that grown-ups hope you'll keep.

S is for the sunshine in your smile; it warms me from head to toe.

T is for the twinkle in your eyes; that sets everyone's hearts aglow.

O is for the October day your spirit came safely to earth.

P is for those puppy dog tails that give you little boy mirth.

H is for the happiness you share with everyone you meet.

E is for the energy with which each morning you playfully greet.

R is for the richness you bring to my life most every day

And I'll pray especially long and hard
That your richness grows in every way.

I love you more each day my son
Although we're far apart.
Remember one thing clearly though,
You are always here in my heart!

*"For this child I prayed;
and the LORD hath given me my petition
which I asked of him:"
1 Samuel 1:27*

CJ Smith Jr.

C is for the caring heart; you show it every day.

J is for your joyful smile shining bright along the way.

S is for the simple way you help others with much cheer,

M is for the many gifts you've given throughout each year.

I is for the intelligence you show in making new LEGO toys,

T is for the way you talk; it truly is a joyful noise.

H is for your handsome face; it shows more wisdom each day.

J is for the joy I felt when you came to earth one May.

R is for the restful peace I pray your days to come,

And I hope you'll have much happiness
In life, in work, in fun.

My love for you may be hard or soft,
But remember my words so true:
As high as the eagles can soar aloft,
So high does my love go for you!

*"For this child I prayed;
and the LORD hath given me my petition which
I asked of him:"*
1 Samuel 1:27

CJ's Gift

For CJ's birthday, every year,
He tells me what he wants so dear.
Sometimes it's big; sometimes it's small,
Sometimes he says, "I don't know at all?"

But this year he says, "Nintendo 64!"
That's what I want even more than more!
He says, "Maybe something 'Nerf', for a second choice",
But, there's a hint of disappointment in his voice.

So, I go to price the 'Nintendo 64!'
It's about the same price at every store.
The thing that bugs me, is they don't give a game,
And one controller comes too; so you pay for the name.

I didn't feel that it was a very good deal,
So, I waited and thought, "If I could just find a 'Steal'!"
But, as I went back again, something else caught my eye,
There were two games in one at a terrific buy!

So, I asked the clerk to explain the toy,
And she said that it works with the games from 'Game Boy'.
"That's great!" I exclaimed, I'll take it; not lend, Oh!
The gift that you've got is a "SUPER NINTENDO!"

"Every good gift and every perfect gift is from above,"
James 1:17a

Fourteen Years

It hardly seems like fourteen years
Since the first time I saw your face.
I was a little scared, you being my first
But in the world you came by God's grace!

You were a miracle then and still are today
A wonderful gift of God's love!
And as you've grown I've watched and prayed
For blessings and mercies from above!

You've grown and matured before my eyes
And developed into quite a young man!
I continue to pray God's grace on your life,
And I hope that you follow His plan!

But now to the joy that your birthday brings;
I've got two small gifts and a surprise!
These two super games for fun here on earth
And a gift to discover the skies!

You probably weren't expecting this gift at all,
But harbored a small ray of hope.
It's not here right now, but soon we will get
From layaway, your new TELESCOPE!

"Blessed be God, even the Father of our Lord Jesus Christ, the Father of mercies, and the God of all comfort;"
2Corinthians 1:3

God's Precious Daughter

Courageous life you live each day;
The world is cold and cruel.

Alive with love for all you see,
You shine bright just like a jewel!

Religion is not a game to you,
You live your life for God!

Obstacles never slow you down,
Through thick and thin you always trod!

Little Lady; Big in heart,
Your precious spirit is set apart!

Miracles are given every day!
Money for food, a raise in pay!

Always loving, living for life!
Always moving through pain and strife!

You are so often filled with laughter,
You are, for sure, God's precious daughter!

"And will be a Father unto you, and ye shall be my sons and daughters, saith the Lord Almighty."
2 Corinthians 6:18

Lost Time

Nothing can ever change what happens in the past.
We forget to call or forget a date and the pain can last
and last.
Was it because we didn't care or didn't want to give?
Usually it's because "The Fast and Furious" is how we
often live!

So, please accept this birthday wish although it's rather late.
We didn't mean to put you off or forget your special date!
We thought about you on that date and due to reason
and rhyme,
We worked and helped and played and talked and only
gained lost time.
Hope you had a Great Birthday! Welcome to the "down"
slide to 40!

*"To every thing there is a season,
and a time to every purpose under the heaven:"
Ecclesiastes 3:1*

Mom

Mom, I'd like to take this time
To tell you how I feel;
The words to come, are from my heart,
And, yes, they're very real.

I want to tell you first of all,
Thanks for being my mom;
And now let me tell you what I think,
Not from Gerry, Kevin, Joanne or Tom.

I used to think you didn't care
Or love me very much;
I thought your work and school and things
Were more important than my school lunch.

As I grew older and moved away,
I thought, to the truth, you were blind;
But the more that I lived and saw more of the world,
I knew it was just in my mind.

You dealt with your life the best that you knew,
And taught me all that you could;
And then you sent me out on my way,
If you could help, you knew that you would.

continued

And now that I have grown still more,
There's something a friend did impart;
The things that you gave me, may have seemed small,
But you gave them straight from your heart.

Now that I've rambled, like you know that I can,
There's something I just have to say;
Mom, I love you with all of my heart!
And, that love grows more everyday!

*"Honour thy father and mother;
which is the first commandment with promise;"
Ephesians 6:2*

Number 11

Another year has come and gone.
More growing you have done.
You've learned and played and hopefully,
You've had a lot of fun!

You're growing older and getting wiser.
Please set your sights on heaven.
And remember that I love you son,
On this birthday number eleven!

*"So teach us to number our days,
that we may apply our hearts unto wisdom."
Psalms 90:12*

One More Year

God has given you one more year,
To love, to laugh, to shed a tear.
He's brought you through to see this day,
So live a life that shows His way.

Your life was full of ups and downs,
God blessed your smiles and lessened your frowns.
His grace has given you strength and joy,
He blessed your womb; boy, girl, boy, girl, boy.

As you celebrate one more year,
Know that the Lord is always near.
Know that He loves you, know that He cares.
Life without Him would be only fair!

"Casting all your care upon him;
for he careth for you."
1 Peter 5:7

Pastors Chris and Carol

As a couple you've been blessed.
To serve the Lord was His request.
So freely of yourselves you've given.
No aspect of your lives have you hidden.

We want to thank you for your caring.
Your wisdom, love and all 'round sharing.
This one more thing we'll say to you.
May God continue to bless you!

*"And he gave some, apostles; and some, prophets;
and some, evangelists; and some, pastors and teachers;
For the perfecting of the saints, for the work of the ministry,
for the edifying of the body of Christ:"
Ephesians 4:11-12*

Sheila

S is for your servant spirit towards God and
towards all others.

H is for your heart of gold, an example for all mothers.

E is for your elegant way that you carry your
light for Christ.

I is for your impish smile that warms us as a light.

L is for your love of Christ, so deep it makes you glow!

A is for allowing Him to use your life; His love towards all
you show!

With each day I come to know
Your love for Christ is deep.
To have a friend so close to God
Blessed is your friendship to keep!

You've brought such joy into my life
I really cannot speak.
You've shown me truly, the love of Christ
Day to day and week to week!

May God bless you each and every day
With His abundance and His love.
And may your heart be forever light
As on the wings of Jesus' Dove!

*"And the servant of the Lord must not strive;
but be gentle unto all men, apt to teach, patient,"*
2 Timothy 2:24

Teenage Present

You were once my baby boy.
You were once a child with a toy.
You were once my only son.
Now you've gone and grown up some!

So, here's the thing
I'm trying to say,
I loved you then
And I love you today!
Keep God in your life
And you'll understand,
That you're growing into
A fine young man!

A birthday prayer
Is what we'll send.
A gift of love
From the world's other end.
My love and Howard's
You'll get in a flash!
And for a teenage present,
You'll get some cash!

*"And it shall come to pass in the last days, saith God,
I will pour out of my Spirit upon all flesh:
and your sons and your daughters shall prophesy,
and your young men shall see visions,
and your old men shall dream dreams:"
Acts 2:17*

The Birthday Party

CJ and Chris in Florida stay.
Their birthdays happen when they're away.
So Mommy will try to be a real smarty,
By giving them a double big birthday party!

*"And thou shalt have joy and gladness;
and many shall rejoice at his birth."*
Luke 1:14

www.ingramcontent.com/pod-product-compliance
Ingram Content Group UK Ltd.
Pitfield, Milton Keynes, MK11 3LW, UK
UKHW041949230426
12048UKWH00008B/239

9 781600 348754